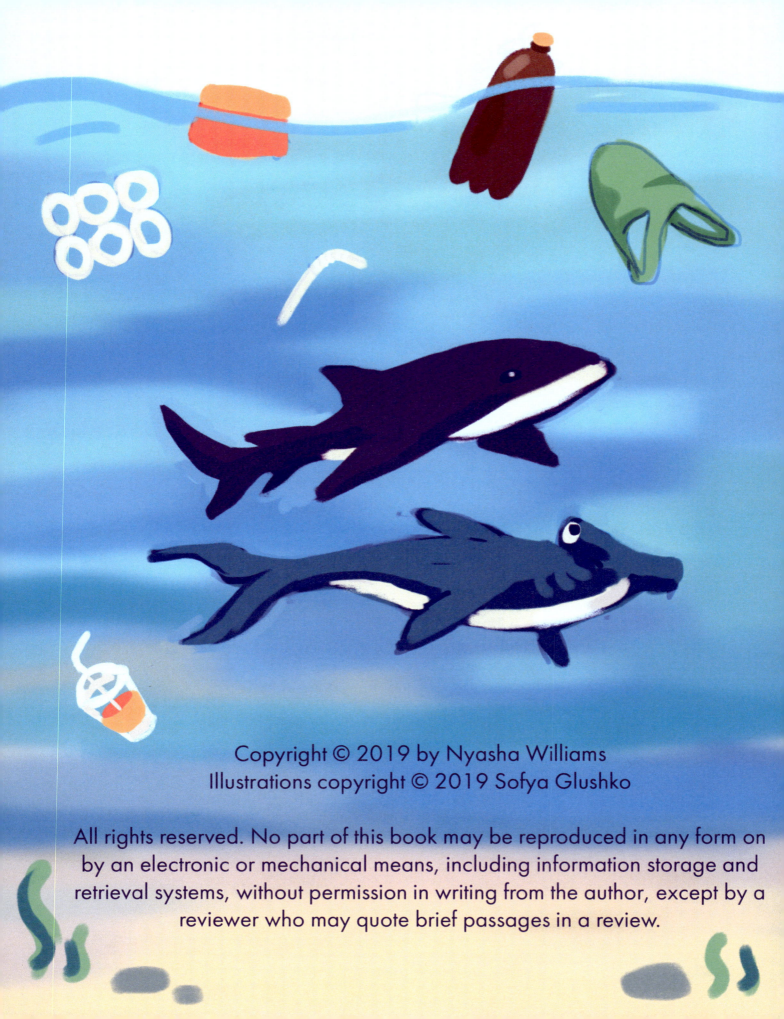

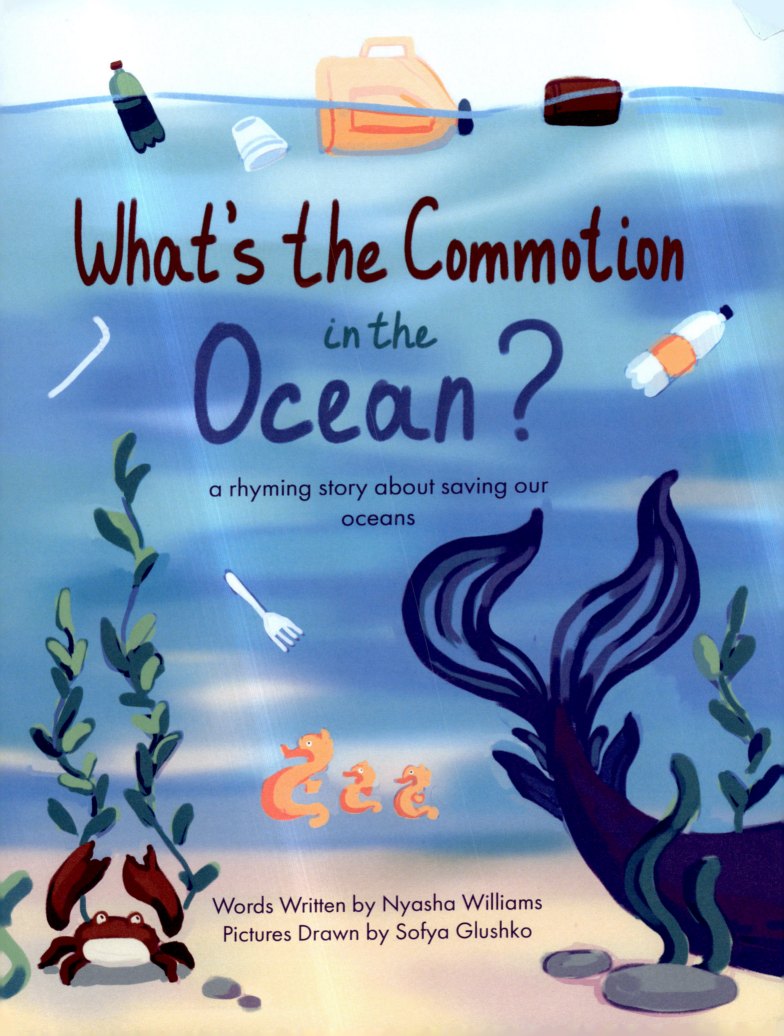

What's the Commotion in the Ocean?

a rhyming story about saving our oceans

Words Written by Nyasha Williams
Pictures Drawn by Sofya Glushko

Do you ever think about the sea? About our oceans and their plea!

Their messages are sent though water spouts, whirlpools, and tidal waves. I am posting this message because we need your aid.

I was born in the water. The oceans and seas are my home. But with the humans treating them so terribly, their future is unsure and unknown.

It's difficult to sum up the oceans worth. Oceans are the most extensive ecosystem here on Earth.

The air we breathe, water we drink,
and food we eat are all gifts to us from
the blue sea beneath.

The ocean blue supports a great deal of life. From sharks to crabs, many animals need the ocean to thrive.

My ocean animal friends cannot tell the difference between plastic and food. They have no clue on what is theirs to be chewed. Causing them to be poisoned by ingesting plastic is putting me in quite the mood.

Fertilizer from lawns and farms, motor oil, and sewage too, then wash down into streams and rivers like a thick, grimey goo.

The goo then flows into the seas and oceans, ending up polluting our waters like a thick, dark potion.

As the number of humans has continued to grow, their demand for seafood has messed up the oceans' status quo.

The way humans are currently fishing is unsustainable. If it keeps happening at the current rates, seafood will become unattainable.

As oil and water do not mix, oil spills put us ocean dwellers in quite a fix. The oil sits on the surface of our home, causing the harm of animals and helping create awful dead zones.

Dead zones are areas of water with low oxygen, with excessive pollution being the origin. In dead zones, marine or plant life is impossible. Humans need to take action against this mess for which they are responsible.

Do you understand my friend? This polluting of the oceans really must come to an end!

What can be done to prevent further ocean pollution? I plan to provide you with some thorough solutions.

Reduce, reuse, and recycle as much as you can, and avoiding using single-use plastic is an excellent start to a plan.

Make sure to indulge in safe and sustainable seafood only.

Partake in gardening by planting trees and greenery boldly.

Take a trip to your nearest beach and help clean up all of the trash you see. It is time for humans to take ownership of your debris.

My time is up as I have done my part, now tell everyone you know about this message from the ocean so that my home can begin a fresh start.

"The sea, once it casts its spell, holds one in its net of wonder forever."
-Jacques Cousteau

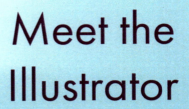

Meet the Illustrator

Sofya Glushko is the character designer and illustrator for the children's book "What's the Commotion in the Ocean?".

Sofya was born in Russia in the northern city of Tomsk. After graduating from school, she moved to Novosibirsk. For several years she was looking for herself in creative professions such as architecture and design, but ultimately her search led her a career in illustrating children's books. Sofya is self-taught and studied drawing at home through online courses. "What's the Commotion in the Ocean?" is Sofya's first commercial project, but far from being the last.

When Sofya isn't drawing, she is a passionate interior decorator and dabbles in sculpture creating.

Meet the Author

Nyasha Williams is a poet, writer, and author of the new children's book, 'What's the Commotion in the Ocean?'.

Nyasha Williams was born in mountain time in Aurora, Colorado, and grew up living intermittently between the United States and South Africa. She received a Bachelors from William Jewell College and a Diploma in Culinary Arts & Wine from Prue Leith Chefs Academy. Following the north wind, she ended up in Baltimore, where she became a multitasking rockstar who aims to inspire and encourage the five-year-olds in her classroom.

Nyasha Williams now lives in Broomfield, Colorado, with her husband. When not writing, Nyasha likes to go on adventures and indulge in fabulous dining experiences.

Ocean Facts

• The north pacific ocean is the most polluted because it contains more than two trillion pieces of plastic floating around it. It is called "The Great Pacific Garbage Patch." The Indian Ocean is the second most polluted ocean. Indian Ocean contains one trillion pieces of plastic.

• Small animals at the bottom of the food chain absorb the chemicals as part of their food. These little animals are eaten by larger animals that again increases the concentration of chemicals. Animals at the top of the hierarchy of food chain have contamination levels millions of times higher than the water in which they live.

• People get contaminated easily by eating contaminated seafood that can cause serious health problems, from cancer to damage to the immune system.

• With each load of laundry, more than 700,000 synthetic microfibers are washed into our waterways. Unlike natural materials such as cotton or wool, these plasticized fibers do not break down. One study showed that synthetic microfibers make up as much as 85 percent of all beach trash.

• Noise pollution generated by shipping and military activity can cause cellular damage to a class of invertebrates that includes jellyfish and anemones. These animals are a vital food source for tuna, sharks, sea turtles, and other creatures.

Most Common Items Found in Ocean Pollution Clean-Ups
1. Cigarettes and filters
2. Food wrappers and containers
3. Caps and lids
4. Tableware
5. Plastic bottles
6. Plastic bags

For more information visit https://theoceanproject.org/